Amazing Nature

Powerful Predators

Tim Knight

Heinemann
LIBRARY

www.heinemann.co.uk/library

Visit our website to find out more information about **Heinemann Library** books.

To order:
☎ Phone 44 (0) 1865 888066
🖷 Send a fax to 44 (0) 1865 314091
🖥 Visit the Heinemann Bookshop at www.heinemann.co.uk/library to browse our catalogue and order online.

First published in Great Britain by Heinemann Library, Halley Court, Jordan Hill, Oxford OX2 8EJ, part of Harcourt Education.
Heinemann is a registered trademark of Harcourt Education Ltd.

Editorial: Jilly Attwood and Claire Throp
Design: David Poole and Geoff Ward
Picture Research: Peter Morris
Production: Séverine Ribierre

Originated by Ambassador Litho Ltd
Printed in China by South China Printing Company

ISBN 0 431 16661 7
07 06 05 04 03
10 9 8 7 6 5 4 3 2 1

British Library Cataloguing in Publication Data
Knight, Tim
Powerful Predators - (Amazing Nature)
591.5'3
A full catalogue record for this book is available from the British Library.

Acknowledgements
The publishers would like to thank the following for permission to reproduce photographs: Ardea pp. **10** (John Daniels), **11** (top) (Ken Lucas), **13** (D. Avon), **17** (Chris Brunskill), **18** (Alan Weaving); FLPA pp. **4** (F. Polking), **15**, **24** (bottom), **25** (Minden Pictures), **16** (C. Carvalho), **19** (Chris Mattison), **20** (Deminsky Photo Ass.), **24** (top) (Mammal Fund Earthviews/Marine); Nature Picture Library p. **7** (Norbert Wu); NHPA pp. **6** (Norbert Wu), **8** (Alan Williams), **9** (James Carmichael Jnr), **11** (bottom) (Daryl Balfour), **12** (David Middleton), **21** (Mirko Stelzner), **22** (Bill Coster), **23** (Stephen Dalton), **26** (T. Kitchin & V. Hust), **27** (Jany Sauvanet); Tim Knight pp. **5**, **14**

Cover photograph of a Nile crocodile reproduced with permission of Nature Picture Library/Richard Kirby.

Every effort has been made to contact copyright holders of any material reproduced in this book. Any omissions will be rectified in subsequent printings if notice is given to the publishers.

Contents

Hunter and hunted 4

Armed and dangerous 6

Sharp eyes 8

The listeners 10

Picking up the scent 12

Touch and feel 14

Stalking 16

Ambush 18

Fishing 20

Lightning strike 22

Brute force 24

Teamwork 26

Fact file 28

Glossary 30

Index 32

Any words appearing in the text in bold, **like this**, are explained in the Glossary.

Hunter and hunted

A **predator** is an animal that hunts and kills other animals for food. Its victim is known as **prey**. Predators have to find, catch and kill their food.

To find food, predators rely on one or more of their sharp senses. A hunting eagle uses its eyesight. A snake 'tastes' the surroundings with its forked tongue. An army ant feels with its **antennae**. A bat-eared fox listens for the sound of insects moving underground. A weasel tracks down prey by following its scent.

Once the prey has been found, it has to be caught. Every kind of predator has its own method of catching food. A cheetah outsprints its prey. A heron spears fish with its sharp beak. Wolves work as a team to bring down a large animal. The bolas spider swings a silk thread, weighted at one end with a blob of glue, and hauls in the insects that stick to it.

Leopards usually kill their prey with a quick bite to the neck.

Some predators eat their prey alive or swallow it whole. For example, hyenas bite chunks from a wounded animal until it dies of shock or loss of blood. Others kill their prey first. Boa constrictors wrap themselves round their victim until it can no longer breathe, then swallow it head first.

Predators come in every shape and size, from tiger sharks to tiger beetles. However different they may look, they all have one thing in common. They are born killers that depend on hunting for survival.

Herons hunt by standing perfectly still in the water until a fish swims close. Then they stab it with their long, sharp beak.

Armed and dangerous

Every **predatory** animal is equipped with a set of tools. Each animal's tool is perfectly suited to the job of catching and killing. This could be a hooked beak, jagged teeth, sharp claws, or even some kind of deadly surprise.

The **venom** of the box jellyfish is lethal. It feeds on shrimps, waiting for them to bump into its tentacles. The jellyfish avoids damage to its tentacles by killing its victim with a deadly poison before it can start struggling. The tentacles, which may be two metres long, are armed with up to 5000 stinging cells. Their venom is powerful enough to kill a man within minutes.

Although this glass jellyfish looks beautiful, its stinging tentacles are deadly weapons.

Tooth

The great white shark has 3000 teeth, which are strong enough to bite through steel. It will attack humans, but usually targets seals and sea lions. It grabs its **prey** from below in a sudden rush, tearing off huge chunks of flesh.

… and claw

Birds of prey, such as eagles and hawks, have strong, needle-sharp claws known as **talons**. The most powerful is the long rear talon. It is this 'killer claw' that pierces the flesh and delivers the fatal blow.

A cat catches prey with its claws. When not in use, the claws are **retracted**. They are protected by a covering that helps to keep them sharp. The cheetah is the only cat that cannot retract its claws, but they do not need to be sharp. Cheetahs trip up their prey from behind, then **suffocate** it by clamping their jaws over its **muzzle**.

The jaws of a great white shark are armed with rows of jagged teeth.

7

Sharp eyes

Some **predators** have excellent eyesight. This helps them to spot **prey** over a long distance, catch sight of sudden movements, or see clearly when there is hardly any light. A soaring buzzard can spot a mouse from a height of 4500 metres.

Humans have one **lens** in each eye and can only look in one direction at a time. Insects have **compound eyes**, each with up to 30,000 separate lenses. Each lens faces a slightly different way. Compound eyes allow a hunting dragonfly to see in all directions at once. They are also excellent at spotting movement, helping the hunter to zero-in on flying insects.

Jumping spiders have four big eyes on their face and four smaller eyes on top of their head. They have better eyesight than any other animal of their size. They hunt like cats, spotting prey from long distances, creeping up, and pouncing on it with the help of their springy legs.

All owls have huge eyes that are fixed in their sockets. An owl has to turn its whole head if it wants to look the other way.

Instead of catching insects in a web, jumping spiders use their sharp eyes to track down their prey.

Giant eyes

The 20-metre long giant squid lives deep in the ocean. It has long, grabbing tentacles covered with powerful suckers, and a sharp, powerful beak for biting. The giant squid also has gigantic eyes, which help it to hunt in the darkest depths of the ocean. Measuring up to 40 centimetres across, they are the largest eyes in the animal kingdom.

The listeners

Hunting by sight alone is impossible if there is not enough light to see. After dark, many **predators** rely on sound instead.

The great grey owl has a saucer-shaped face covered with extra fine feathers. This **facial disc** helps to collect sound waves and direct them into the owl's ears. It also has one ear higher than the other, which helps it to pinpoint exactly where a noise is coming from. If its target is out of sight beneath snow or leaves, the owl hovers above the sound. This gives its ears time to focus on the correct spot before it pounces.

Animal radar

Dolphins hunt using **echolocation**. They make a clicking sound, which produces an echo when it bounces back off nearby objects. The length of time taken for the sound to bounce back tells the dolphins exactly where the invisible object is. They can even tell what size it is. This sound system allows dolphins to catch fish in muddy water or in total darkness.

Insect-eating bats can hunt in total darkness. They use their ears and nose like radar dishes to locate the position of their prey.

The fennec is a small desert fox, found in the Sahara.

Fox links

The fennec fox has massive ears. These help it to pick up the tiny sounds made by the insect prey that it hunts at night. The bat-eared fox also uses its huge ears to listen for underground noises made by its **prey**, and then quickly digs them out with its strong claws.

A family of bat-eared foxes basks in the evening sun before setting out to hunt.

11

Picking up the scent

Many **predators** rely on a keen sense of smell to track down a meal. **Mammals** smell with their nose, snakes flick out their tongues, and insects use their **antennae**.

The shape of a mammal's face usually gives a clue about how it finds **prey**. Coyotes, bears, foxes and jackals, which hunt by smell, all have long snouts. The extra space inside their nose makes room for more smelling equipment. Polar bears can sniff out a seal up to 30 kilometres away.

Sharks have a remarkable sense of smell. They can smell blood up to half a kilometre away. Hammerhead sharks are often the first to find an injured fish. They have a nostril at each end of their hammer-shaped head. As soon as they scent prey, they swing their head from side to side, smelling the water. Once the smell is equally strong in both nostrils, they swim full speed ahead.

A brown bear sniffs the air, trying to 'read' the smells carried on the breeze.

A grass snake flicks out its tongue and uses it like a nose to pick up the scent of small animals.

Most snakes taste the air with their tongue. One group of snakes hunts with the aid of an even more powerful sense. Pit vipers are named after the two small 'pits' just in front of their eyes. Although these pits look like an extra pair of nostrils, they are sensitive to heat, not smell. They pick up the tiniest rise in temperature – a fraction of one degree – caused by the body heat of nearby prey. The pits help to point the snake in the right direction. In total darkness, the pit viper glides silently towards its target and delivers a deadly bite.

Touch and feel

Some **predators** hunt by 'feeling' their way around. Foraging ants, for example, explore with their **antennae** until they bump into something they can eat. The Venus flytrap is the closest thing to a predator in the plant kingdom. It snaps up insects that touch the hair triggers on its hinged leaves.

Starry-nosed

The star-nosed mole has a ring of fleshy **feelers** around its nose that wave about like a bunch of fingers. Like all moles, it has very poor eyesight. Moving through a dark tunnel, it searches for **prey** by waving these feelers rapidly from side to side. The feelers can touch ten different objects in a single second. If the feelers touch a worm, the mole snaps it up in an instant.

The leaves of a Venus flytrap will only snap shut if an insect touches the same hair trigger twice.

A seal's whiskers help it to follow the 'trail' left behind by a swimming fish. Their finely tuned whiskers pick up tiny vibrations along the path taken by the fish. This allows them to hunt in murky water where their eyes are useless. The harbour seal can track a fish up to 180 metres away.

Seals and otters use their whiskers to 'feel for' prey in muddy or dark water.

Stalking

Once a **predator** has located a meal, the next step is to catch it. Chasing **prey** over a long distance burns up a lot of energy, so some animals save their strength by 'stalking'. This involves sneaking up on their prey, delaying their attack until it is within striking range. The closer a predator comes to its victim before being spotted, the better its chances of making a kill.

The barn owl is a silent night hunter. Its fluffy feathers help to muffle the sound of its wings. The front edge of its flight feathers also has a fringe like a very fine comb. These feathers deaden the sound of air passing across them. The silent flight prevents the owl's prey from hearing its approach, and also helps the owl's own hearing.

Polar bears often swim underwater towards their prey and resurface when they are close enough to launch a surprise attack.

A stalking tiger crouches low and inches forward, one paw at a time. The tiger's striped coat breaks up the outline of its body. This makes it harder to see as it moves through the undergrowth.

The Ethiopian wolf hunts giant mole-rats by sneaking up commando-style. Crawling on its belly, it freezes whenever the mole-rat looks up, then creeps forward when its back is turned. As long as the wolf keeps still, it won't be spotted, because mole-rats have poor eyesight.

Deadly snail

Cone shells are deadly ocean snails. They stalk without appearing to move at all. After sniffing out a nearby meal, the cone shell unravels a long hose. At its tip is a **radula**, a ribbon-shaped tongue covered with tiny teeth. Once its prey is within range, a tiny, poison-filled harpoon shoots out from the end of the cone shell's tongue. The victim is killed instantly, and reeled back into the shell.

Ambush

Rather than going in search of their **prey**, some **predators** prefer to sit tight and wait for a meal to come to them. The key to success is surprise. Some predators may **ambush** their victims by setting traps, or hide by blending in with their surroundings.

The trap-door spider spends the day in a silk-lined burrow. It is protected by a lid made from silk and bits of material that match the surrounding soil. After dark, it lifts the lid slightly and pokes out its front legs. When an insect walks by, the spider grabs it and drags it inside.

The legs and body of the orchid mantis are decorated with a cloak of false flower petals. The disguise is so perfect that **nectar**-feeding insects land among the false petals. They fly straight into the deadly trap.

The waiting game

The gaboon viper spends most of its time lying completely still, somewhere along the path normally taken by its prey. The snake's markings exactly match the pattern of the leaves and sunlight on the forest floor. This **camouflage** makes it almost invisible. When its victim is in range, the snake strikes with amazing speed. It injects deadly **venom** that is powerful enough to kill a man in 15 minutes.

The fangs of the gaboon viper measure up to 55 millimetres and are the longest of any snake in the world.

Fishing

Instead of just waiting for a meal to appear, some hunters try fishing. They coax their **prey** within striking range by tempting it with **bait**.

The **aquatic** genet is a cat-like **carnivore** from central Africa. It hunts by quiet forest pools and attracts fish by gently patting the water surface. When the fish arrive to find out whether some food has fallen into the pool, the genet quickly grabs them in its mouth.

The alligator snapper turtle lies on the river bottom with its jaws wide open. Attached to the inside of its mouth is a small piece of flesh that looks like a bright red worm. When a fish tries to grab the wiggling bait, the turtle simply snaps shut its mouth.

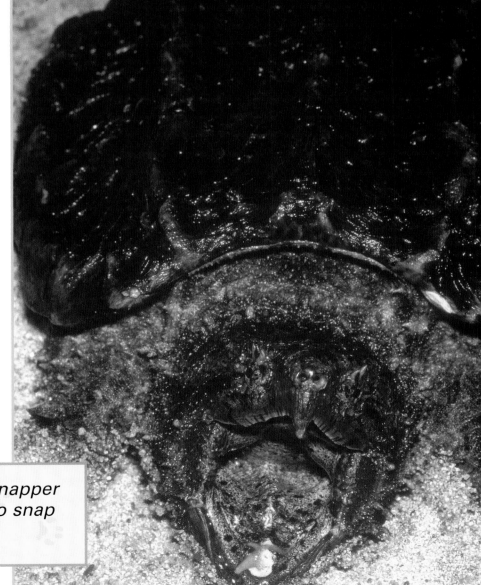

The jaws of the alligator snapper turtle are strong enough to snap off a human finger.

Fishing out of water

One small **predator** from Costa Rica, the assassin bug, uses its leftovers as bait. It grabs a termite and sucks out its insides. The bug then dangles the empty **carcass** next to the entrance to the termites' home. When a worker termite appears and tries to tidy away the body to keep the nest clean, the killer bug grabs it, sucks it dry, and starts fishing for its next victim.

Assassin bugs catch other insects by grabbing them with their front legs. They bite into their prey and suck out the juicy bits.

Lightning strike

Once a hunter is close enough to its target, it must attack quickly before it is discovered. A crouching tiger or leopard uses its powerful leg muscles to pounce, exploding from its hiding place. The cheetah relies on pure speed. It is the fastest animal on four legs and can sprint after its **prey** at speeds of up to 100 kilometres per hour.

A fish called the great barracuda takes less than a second to reach its maximum speed of 100 kilometres per hour. It travels through the water like a bullet and attacks its prey with razor-sharp teeth.

When hunting gannets find a shoal of fish, they dive-bomb their targets at speeds up to 150 kilometres per hour. The birds' skulls have built-in crash helmets to protect them as they smash into the water.

*A striking rattlesnake lunges forward at a speed of 3 metres per second with its jaws gaping wide. It injects a lethal dose of **venom** with its needle-sharp fangs before its victim is even aware of the danger.*

Fastest bird

The fastest of all birds is the peregrine falcon. It flies high above its prey, then plunges down at top speed. It tucks in its wings so that its body is as **streamlined** as possible. By the end of its dive, the peregrine may be travelling at almost 300 kilometres per hour.

The chameleon is a far less energetic hunter, but it strikes even more quickly. When an insect lands within range, the lizard shoots out a long, sticky tongue and snaps up its victim in the blink of an eye.

Brute force

Predators that hunt large **prey** need strength to overpower their catch. The harpy eagle is the strongest bird of prey in the world. With **talons** as big as a grizzly bear's claws and as powerful as a hyena's jaws, it can crush a monkey's skull as if it was an eggshell.

This young harpy eagle will grow to become the most powerful flying predator in its forest home.

Eagle links

There are three kinds of giant eagle in the world: the harpy eagle lives in the rainforests of South America; Africa is the home of the crowned eagle; the monkey-eating eagle is found in the Philippines. All three have large crests, massive beaks and powerful talons. They all hit their prey with such force that it is often killed instantly.

The Philippine monkey-eating eagle uses its enormous beak to rip open its prey.

The world's largest lizard, the Komodo dragon, grows up to 3 metres long. It hunts by **ambushing** deer and wild pigs. It seizes them in its vice-like jaws and rips them open. Once bitten, an animal is doomed even if it escapes. The wound becomes infected by deadly **bacteria** from the lizard's mouth. The Komodo dragon then uses its strong sense of smell to track down its dying prey.

Reticulated pythons and anacondas are the world's largest snakes. They can be almost 10 metres long. They kill by wrapping their coils tightly around their prey so that it cannot breathe. This is known as **constriction**. The hinged jaws of the anaconda allow it to swallow prey five times the width of its own mouth.

A fully grown Komodo dragon looks as though it belongs in a film about dinosaurs.

25

Teamwork

Even for the most powerful **predator**, tackling large **prey** can be a dangerous business, particularly if it is hunting alone. Killer whales join forces to attack blue whales ten times their own size. Wolves can only bring down a 500-kilogram moose by working as a pack.

The most successful pack hunters in Africa are wild dogs. They rely on stamina and teamwork. After choosing their target, they chase it patiently. They can keep going at a steady pace of up to 50 kilometres per hour. As their prey tires and slows down, the leading dogs take turns to snap and tear at its rear. When it is exhausted, the pack closes in and rips it apart.

Hunting in teams reduces the risk of injury and increases the chances of making a kill. Sharing the meal with the rest of the pack is a small price for each wolf to pay.

Tiny terrors

Even tiny predators can be terrifying when they work together. Army ants march through the South American rainforest in long columns, killing and eating anything in their path. They feel for prey with their antennae, then swarm all over it. No animal is safe from attack. An ant army working as a team is more dangerous than a single large predator.

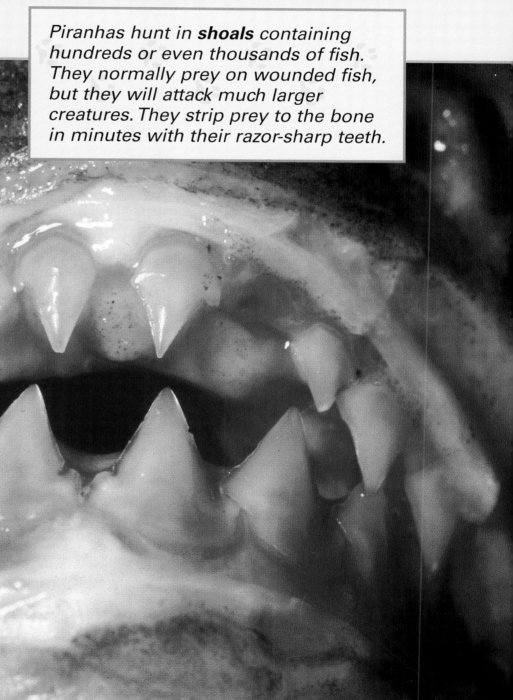

*Piranhas hunt in **shoals** containing hundreds or even thousands of fish. They normally prey on wounded fish, but they will attack much larger creatures. They strip prey to the bone in minutes with their razor-sharp teeth.*

Fact file

The taipan is the most **venomous** snake in the world. It is found only in Australia. One bite from a taipan would produce enough venom to kill over 15,000 mice.

A crocodile drowns its **prey** by dragging it underwater and spinning over and over again. This is known as the 'crocodile roll' or 'death roll'.

Some sharks can smell one part of blood in 100 million parts of water.

The biggest recorded great white shark was 7 metres long and weighed 3200 kilograms.

The world's heaviest snake is the anaconda, weighing 250 kilograms. The middle of its body is almost as thick as a tractor tyre.

An average fully-grown polar bear weighs the same as seven men.

Lions are the only cats that hunt together. This allows them to tackle massive prey, including buffalo and even elephants weighing 1000 kilograms or more.

The largest piranha **shoals** contain up to 20,000 fish.

A colony of army ants may contain over half a million individual insects.

Electric eels have an in-built battery and their bodies produce electricity. They kill their prey by giving it a massive electric shock.

The reticulated python sometimes catches such large prey that it does not need to eat again for two years.

The fringe-lipped bat lives in Central America. It listens for the sound of singing mud-puddle frogs, and swoops down to grab them out of their ponds.

Green-backed herons in a Japanese park saw visitors throwing bread to the fish in the lake. After watching this, they learned to pick up the bread themselves, drop it in the water, and spear the fish that swam up to eat it.

The larva of the ant-lion digs a **funnel**-shaped hole in the ground. It covers the steep sides with loose grains of sand. When ants and other insects fall into the trap, the slippery slopes stop them climbing out again. The ant-lion buries itself at the bottom of the trap, with only its jaws sticking out, ready to grab whatever falls into the pit.

The African clawless otter uses its paws like hands, feeling for prey in mud and cloudy water with its sensitive 'fingers'.

The wolverine is the largest weasel in the world. It is built like a miniature bear and is strong enough to kill a reindeer five times its own size.

Glossary

ambush lie hidden ready to make a surprise attack

antenna (plural is **antennae**) feeler on the head of an insect

aquatic living in water

bacteria tiny forms of life that help food to rot, but can also cause disease

bait object used to attract prey

camouflage disguise that helps an animal to hide

carcass body of a dead animal

carnivore meat eater

compound eye (insect) eye made up of many separate lenses

constriction killing by squeezing so tightly that the victim cannot breathe

echolocation technique used by bats and dolphins to hunt in the dark

facial disc covering of extra fine feathers on an owl's face

feelers animal parts that are sensitive to touch

funnel object with a wide opening that gradually narrows into a tube

lens (plural is **lenses**) transparent part of the eye that gathers rays of light

mammal animal that feeds its young on milk

muzzle long snout with nose and mouth at tip

nectar sugary liquid produced by flowers

predator animal that hunts and kills for food

prey animal that is killed and eaten by predators

radula saw-like tongue of, for example, a slug or snail

retracted drawn back inside a protective cover

shoal large group of fish

streamlined smooth and pointed to improve movement through air or water

suffocate kill by covering the mouth and nose

talon long, needle-sharp claw

venom poison

venomous poisonous

Index

ambush 18–19
ants 4, 14, 27, 28, 29
assassin bugs 21

barracudas 22
bats 10, 29
bears 12, 16, 28

chameleons 23
cheetahs 4, 7, 22
cone shells 17
crocodiles 28

dolphins 10

eagles 4, 7, 24
echolocation 10
eels 29
eyesight 8–9, 14

falcons 23
feeling and touch 14–15
fishing for prey 20–1, 29
foxes 4, 11, 12

gannets 22
genets 20

hearing 10–11
herons 4, 5, 29
hyenas 5

jellyfish 6

leopards 4, 22
lions 28, 29

moles 14

owls 8, 10, 16

pack hunters 26–7, 29
piranhas 27, 28
plants 14, 18

seals 15
sharks 7, 12, 28
smell, sense of 12–13
snakes 4, 5, 12, 13, 19, 23,
    28, 29
speed of attack 22–3
spiders 4, 8, 9, 18
squid 9
stalking 16–17
strength 24

talons 7, 24
teeth 7, 27
tigers 17, 22
turtles 20

venom 6, 17, 19, 28
Venus flytrap 14

weasels 4, 29
whales 26
wild dogs 26
wolves 4, 17, 26

Titles in the *Amazing Nature* series include:

Amazing Nature
Dramatic Displays
Tim Knight

Hardback   0 431 16652 8

Amazing Nature
Fantastic Feeders
Tim Knight

Hardback   0 431 16650 1

Amazing Nature
Ferocious Fighters
Tim Knight

Hardback   0 431 16651 X

Amazing Nature
Incredible Life Cycles
Tim Knight

Hardback   0 431 16662 5

Amazing Nature
Magnificent Movers
Tim Knight

Hardback   0 431 16660 9

Amazing Nature
Marvellous Migrators
Tim Knight

Hardback   0 431 16653 6

Amazing Nature
Powerful Predators
Tim Knight

Hardback   0 431 16661 7

Amazing Nature
Super Survivors
Tim Knight

Hardback   0 431 16663 3

Find out about the other titles in this series on our website www.heinemann.co.uk/library